Working
in the
Wild

Written by Nancy O'Connor
and Kerrie Shanahan

Flying Start
to Literacy®

Contents

Chapter 3

Introduction

Millions of people visit national parks every year. It is a great way to enjoy nature, take photographs, get exercise and learn about the history of an area.

But sometimes, visitors can cause problems. They sometimes leave litter or try to feed the wild animals. They may trample on the plant life or pollute the lakes and streams.

Park rangers believe it is their duty to protect the park from the people and to protect the people from the park and its wildlife. It can be hard to allow the public to use these precious areas for recreation while still preserving nature. Still, it is a job that park rangers love doing.

Chapter 1

Denali National Park

The tallest mountain in North America is in Denali National Park in Alaska. This park covers about 2.5 million hectares, which is about one third of the size of Tasmania. In the winter, the park is buried in snow. Temperatures can get as cold as minus 40 degrees Celsius.

This huge park is home to bears, moose, caribou and other wild animals. Each year, more than 600,000 people visit the park, in both summer and winter.

Alaska
● **Denali National Park**

Canada

United States
of America

Dogsled driver

Jen Raffaeli is a park ranger at Denali and is in charge of the National Park Service's only team of sled dogs.

As the driver of the dogsled, she is called the **chief musher**. During the snowy winter, dogsleds are a better way to travel than snowmobiles. Snowmobile engines might not start in such cold temperatures.

Jen works with 31 Alaskan huskies. The dogs pull the sleds that carry park rangers and equipment through the icy wilderness. Jen and her team help other park rangers maintain trails and patrol for **poachers**, who illegally hunt for moose, bears and other wildlife.

They also **monitor glaciers** and, for winter visitors, report on ice and snow conditions in remote areas of the park.

Summer duties

In the summer, Jen manages the kennels and talks to park visitors about the important role of sled dogs in Denali.

She also takes care of the newborn puppies. The one-year-old puppies get to run loose alongside the experienced dogs when Jen takes them out for training sessions. The sled she uses for summer training is on wheels since there is no snow.

On being a park ranger

How did Jen get such a fun and exciting job?

Before being hired as chief musher in 2010, she worked for two years as a regular park ranger in Denali Park.

Jen's love of animals was an important qualification. But she had also spent many years working as a wilderness guide and teaching others about the outdoors. This experience made Jen perfect for the job.

Chapter 2
Raine Island National Park

Raine Island National Park is a small island right at the top of the Great Barrier Reef in Queensland, Australia. It is an important place for wildlife, and only scientists and park rangers are allowed to visit the island.

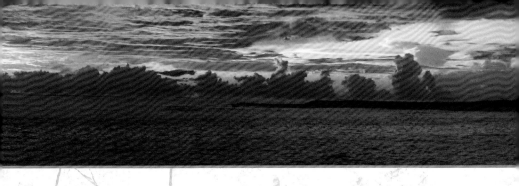

Each year, thousands of female green sea turtles come to Raine Island to lay their eggs. These turtles swim from faraway places and somehow all arrive at the same tiny island, where they themselves once hatched out of eggs.

Green turtles are listed as vulnerable, which means they are at a high risk of becoming endangered. One of the main jobs of the park rangers and scientists who work at Raine Island is to protect the turtles.

Raine Island
National Park

Australia

The problem

Dr Andrew Dunstan is a scientist who works at Raine Island National Park. When he first began working there, the green turtles that nested on the island were in trouble. The problem was caused by the rising water levels around the island. The newly-laid eggs were being covered by seawater and washed away.

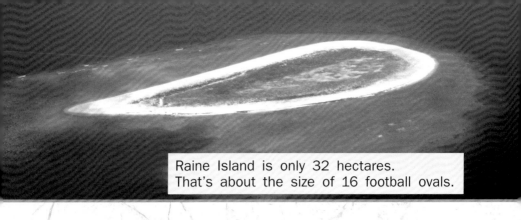

Raine Island is only 32 hectares.
That's about the size of 16 football ovals.

The changes in water levels also meant there were fewer sandy beaches for the turtles to dig nests and lay their eggs. And with fewer beaches, more adult turtles were dying. Up to 2,000 turtles were dying each year.

Saving the turtles

Andrew and his team knew that they had to do something to protect the green sea turtles and their eggs.

During nesting season, Andrew and his team looked for turtles in trouble. Sometimes they found turtles lying on their backs, unable to move. They flipped the turtles over and helped them get back to the ocean.

A park ranger watches as a green sea turtle makes its way back to the ocean.

A long journey

The green sea turtles that nest on Raine Island swim from faraway places like Vanuatu and Indonesia. Some swim up to 2,600 kilometres. That's further than the distance between Sydney and Cairns.

Park rangers look for nests so they can protect the eggs and hatchlings.

Some turtles were dying from exhaustion as they searched for a sandy spot to dig their nests, or by getting stuck in rocky **crevices** that were no longer covered with sand. The rangers used a special sled to help these turtles back to the water.

Fixing the habitat

Andrew and his team have created
a new beach where the turtles
can dig nests and lay eggs. They
did this by relocating loads of sand
from other parts of the island, to
make a wide sandy beach that is
high above the tide level.

The island has also been made safer.
Fences have been built around dangerous
rocky areas so that the turtles can't fall
off the small cliffs.

Park rangers count hatchlings from a green sea turtle nest.

Turtle research

Andrew studies the green turtles that nest on Raine Island. He counts the number of eggs that are laid and the number of turtles that hatch.

Some of the turtles are fitted with tracking devices so that Andrew can gather data and learn more about them. This information can then be used to continue to protect the vulnerable green sea turtle.

Chapter 3

Abel Tasman National Park

Abel Tasman National Park is the smallest national park in New Zealand, but it is one of the most beautiful. The park is near the city of Nelson on the South Island, and it has both coastal and forest areas.

This national park is a popular tourist destination. People visit the park to snorkel, kayak, hike or camp. Many of the visitors come to the park to experience one of New Zealand's "Great Walks" – the Abel Tasman Coast Track. On this walk, people can see **pristine** bays, thick forests and impressive **granite** rock formations.

Summer is the busiest time at the park, and rangers spend time talking with visitors about weather forecasts and tide times. They also talk about the park's history and the many plants and animals that can be found there.

Abel Tasman National Park

New Zealand

Staying safe in the park

Sarah Tunnicliffe is a trainee ranger at Abel Tasman National Park. She makes sure that visitors know the park's rules. This keeps the visitors safe and also protects the park.

Sarah makes sure that the visitors to the park have campsite bookings.

Sarah and the other rangers monitor the weather conditions and tide times and discuss these with people visiting the park. It is important that people going on hikes or kayaking trips are aware of what weather to expect, especially if storms are on the way.

Some parts of the Abel Tasman Coast Track are on the beach. Hikers must know the times of low and high tides, so an unexpected high tide doesn't cut them off.

Wildlife

Sarah educates visitors to the park about the wildlife they might see. A recent addition to the park were four new kākā chicks. The kākā bird is almost extinct in the wild, so when the chicks hatched it was very exciting.

An unusual rescue

As all park rangers know, every day as a park ranger is different, and you never know what might happen next. This was definitely true for Sarah when a pod of about 600 pilot whales **beached** themselves on the coast and became stranded.

Sarah worked with other park rangers from all around the country, as well as many volunteers, to help the beached whales. They worked hard to rescue as many whales as possible. It is estimated that about 400 whales were saved. All in a day's work for park rangers like Sarah.

Conclusion

The work that park rangers do is as varied as the parks where they work. Some rangers clear trails, and some count sea turtles. Others may be helicopter pilots who rescue visitors if they are in danger. Rangers may also be firefighters or scientists.

What they all have in common is a love of the natural environment and wild animals, and a passion to share their knowledge with you.

Glossary

beached hauled up or stranded on a beach

chief musher a person who drives a dogsled

crevices small, narrow openings in rocks

glaciers large bodies of ice moving slowly down a slope or valley

granite a type of rock that is very hard; it is often used for buildings and for monuments

monitor to keep track of or to watch for a special purpose

poachers people who steal animals from the wild

pristine in a natural state, not changed by people

Index